I See the Sea

TEACHING HOMOPHONES

BY MARY LINDEEN

The Child's World®
childsworld.com

Published by The Child's World®
1980 Lookout Drive • Mankato, MN 56003-1705
800-599-READ • www.childsworld.com

ACKNOWLEDGMENTS
The Child's World®: Mary Swensen, Publishing Director
Red Line Editorial: Editorial direction and production
The Design Lab: Design

Photographs ©: Alinute Silzeviciute/Shutterstock Images, cover
(left), 2, 14-15; Viktor Gladkov/Shutterstock Images, cover
(background), 1; Perfect Gui/Shutterstock Images, 4; Olga
Danylenko/Shutterstock Images, 4–5; Shutterstock Images, 6,
9, 12, 13; Steve Mann/Shutterstock Images, 8; Tony Campbell/
Shutterstock Images, 10–11

ISBN 9781503808409
LCCN 2015958428

Printed in the United States of America
Mankato, MN
June, 2016
PA02304

ABOUT THE AUTHOR
Mary Lindeen is a writer, editor, former
elementary school teacher, and parent. She
has written more than 100 books for children.
She specializes in early literacy instruction and
creating books for young readers.

Homophones are words that sound the same but have different meanings. Look for **homophones** in this book. You will find them in **bold** type.

I take a ride in a
plain plane.
I get a **peek** of a
snowy mountain **peak**.

4

I **see** the **sea**.

I almost **missed** it in the **mist**.

I stay **in** an **inn** to get some sleep.
The **maid** has not **made** the bed.

I find some **fur** in a
fir tree.
I look up into the
branches for a
bare bear.

I step in a **hole** and hurt my **whole** foot.

I will have to wait for my **heel** to **heal**.

I **plant** a **plant**.
I **hear** the sounds of
nature **here**.

Did you hear these homophones?

bare/bear	made/maid
fir/fur	missed/mist
heal/heel	peak/peek
hear/here	plain/plane
hole/whole	plant/plant
in/inn	sea/see

To Learn More

IN THE LIBRARY
Barretta, Gene. *Dear Deer: A Book of Homophones*. New York: Square Fish, 2010.

Coffelt, Nancy. *Aunt Ant Leaves through the Leaves: A Story with Homophones and Homonyms*. New York: Holiday House, 2012.

Felix, Rebecca. *A Pair of Pears*. North Mankato, MN: Amicus, 2014.

ON THE WEB
Visit our Web site for links about homophones:
childsworld.com/links

Note to Parents, Teachers, and Librarians: We routinely verify our Web links to make sure they are safe and active sites. So encourage your readers to check them out!